OCEANS

A Buddy Book
by
Fran Howard

ABDO
Publishing Company

VISIT US AT
www.abdopublishing.com

Published by ABDO Publishing Company, 4940 Viking Drive, Edina, Minnesota 55435.

Copyright © 2007 by Abdo Consulting Group, Inc. International copyrights reserved in all countries. No part of this book may be reproduced in any form without written permission from the publisher. Buddy Books™ is a trademark and logo of ABDO Publishing Company.

Printed in the United States.

Edited by: Sarah Tieck
Contributing Editor: Michael P. Goecke
Graphic Design: Brady Wise
Image Research: Deb Coldiron, Maria Hosley, Heather Sagisser, Brady Wise
Photographs: Animals Animals, Corbis, Digital Stock, Minden Pictures, Photodisc, photos.com

Library of Congress Cataloging-in-Publication Data

Howard, Fran, 1953-
    Oceans / Fran Howard.
        p. cm. — (Habitats)
    Includes bibliographical references and index.
    ISBN 1-59679-781-9 (10 digit ISBN)
    ISBN 978-1-59679-781-9 (13 digit ISBN)
        1. Marine biology—Juvenile literature. I. Title. II. Series: Habitats (Edina, Minn.)

QH91.16H69 2006.
578.77—dc22

                                                          2005031681

TABLE OF CONTENTS

WHAT IS AN OCEAN?

Oceans have waves.

Oceans are big bodies of salt water. They are the biggest bodies of water on Earth.

Oceans are also habitats. Habitats are the places where plants and animals find food, water, and places to live. Different plants and animals live in different habitats.

There are many plants and animals that live in the world's oceans.

Fish live in the ocean.

WHERE ARE OCEANS FOUND?

A view of the Pacific coast.

The Earth has five oceans. All five oceans are connected. They cover about 70 percent of the Earth's surface. Oceans contain most of the water on Earth.

A beach on the Pacific Ocean.

The Pacific Ocean is the largest ocean in the world. The Arctic Ocean is the smallest.

The other oceans are the Atlantic Ocean, the Indian Ocean, and the Southern Ocean. Parts of the Southern and Arctic oceans are covered in ice.

PLANTS OF
THE OCEANS

The top layer of the ocean is sunlit. The bottom layers are dark. Most plants and animals live in the sunlit zone. But, there are plants and animals that live in the deepest, darkest parts of the ocean.

Fields of sea grass grow underwater. Sea grass supplies food and shelter for animals.

Plankton are small plants and animals that float in the oceans. Many animals eat plankton.

Some trees even grow in shallow ocean waters. These are called mangrove trees. Mangrove trees offer food and shelter for animals.

This ocean plant captures plankton.

FISH AND OTHER OCEAN ANIMALS

A clown fish with a sea anemone.

Many interesting animals live in the oceans. The clown fish is an orange and white striped fish. Clown fish live closely with sea anemones.

Sea anemones look like flowers, but they eat fish. They have colorful tentacles that look like fingers.

An anemone

Clown fish and sea
anemones help each other.

Sea anemones hide clown fish. Clown
fish clean sea anemones and protect
them from certain fish.

The octopus lives on the ocean floor. An octopus has eight arms called tentacles. Sometimes, it squirts dark ink at its enemies.

An octopus

Sea turtles are different from land turtles. Sea turtles cannot hide in their shells like other turtles. Sea turtles also have flippers designed to help them swim. And, some sea turtles eat sea grass. Others eat fish.

A sea turtle

Sea turtles are good swimmers.

Some sea turtles eat jellyfish.

A hammerhead shark

Sharks are some of the biggest fish in the ocean. Sharks are good hunters. They eat fish and turtles.

Some sharks have heads shaped like a hammer. These sharks are called hammerheads. Hammerhead sharks live in warm oceans.

Sharks have teeth that grow in rows.
They use their teeth to eat fish and turtles.

Sharks hunt for their food.

Penguins are ocean birds. But they cannot fly. They have flippers instead of wings. Penguins use their flippers to swim through the water.

Penguins live in the southern part of the world. They spend time on land and in the water. Most penguins swim in icy oceans.

A penguin's body is designed to help keep it warm.

Mammals Of
The Oceans

Manatees in the ocean.

Some **mammals** live in the oceans, too. Manatees are mammals that live in warm oceans. Manatees are also called sea cows.

Manatees move very slowly underwater.

Manatees can stay underwater for 20 minutes. Manatees eat sea grass and other plants found in the ocean.

Dolphins are **mammals** that live in oceans, too. They live and hunt in groups.

Dolphins can dive.

Dolphins can jump.

A beluga whale

Whales are the biggest **mammals** in the ocean. The beluga whale lives in the icy Arctic Ocean. Beluga whales are slow swimmers.

Killer whales are bigger than belugas.
Killer whales hunt other whales, dolphins,
and turtles.

A killer whale

Polar bears hunt for food in the water.

Polar bears have white fur. It matches the snow.

The polar bear's body is designed to help keep it warm.

Polar bears spend a lot of time swimming in the Arctic Ocean. Polar bears eat seals. Sometimes, they even eat beluga whales trapped in the ice.

WHY ARE OCEAN HABITATS IMPORTANT?

Some people sail on the ocean waters.

People and animals need oceans.
People eat fish caught in the ocean.

People also use oceans as waterways for boats. Boats move people and things from place to place. Oceans supply people with water.

People and animals need oxygen to breathe. Ocean plants produce oxygen. Ocean plants make 71 percent of the Earth's oxygen.

An ocean wave

Without oceans, the earth could become too cold or too hot. Oceans cool the land in winter and warm it in summer.

Ocean animals and plants need each other. Together they form a **food chain**. Even the smallest plants and animals are part of the food chain.

Ocean plants and animals cannot live without their habitat.

Baleen Whale   Krill   Plankton

OCEANS

- Kelp grows from the ocean floor. It can be more than 200 feet (60 m) tall. This is taller than most trees.

- Earthquakes can sometimes cause giant waves called tsunamis. Tsunamis are very fast. The waves can travel for thousands of miles. Sometimes tsunamis harm people and cities.

- There are **fossils** in the ocean.

- The ocean floor shifts and moves all the time.

- There are mountains and volcanoes beneath the ocean.

IMPORTANT WORDS

food chain the order in which plants and animals feed on each other.

fossil the remains of a very old animal or plant commonly found in the ground. A fossil can be a bone, a footprint, or any trace of life.

mammal most living things that belong to this special group have hair, give birth to live babies, and make milk to feed their babies.

WEB SITES

Would you like to learn more about **oceans**? Please visit ABDO Publishing Company on the World Wide Web to find Web site links about **oceans**. These links are routinely monitored and updated to provide the most current information available.

www.abdopublishing.com

INDEX